Get to Know Wedges

by Jennifer Christiansen

Crabtree Publishing Company

www.crabtreebooks.com

Crabtree Publishing Company

www.crabtreebooks.com

Author: Jennifer Christiansen
Editors: Molly Aloian, Reagan Miller, Crystal Sikkens
Project coordinator: Robert Walker
Prepress technicians: Ken Wright, Margaret Amy Salter
Production coordinator: Margaret Amy Salter
Cover design: Samara Parent
Coordinating editor: Chester Fisher
Series and project editor: Penny Dowdy
Project manager: Kumar Kunal (Q2AMEDIA)
Art direction: Dibakar Acharjee (Q2AMEDIA)
Design: Ritu Chopra (Q2AMEDIA)
Photo research: Farheen Aadil (Q2AMEDIA)

Illustrations:
Q2AMedia Art Bank: p. 6, 7, 10, 11, 14, 15, 16, 18, 19, 22, 23, 26, 27

Photographs:
Alamy: Bernie Epstein: p. 17
Helene Rogers/Art Directors: p. 12
Corbis: Cultura: p. 24; David Gubernick: p. 28
Ingram photo objects: p. 4 (lever)
Istockphoto: Clayton Hansen: p. 4 (wheel and axle);
    Randy Mayes: p. 25
Mark Vivian/Mary Evans Picture Library: p. 29
Photographers Direct: Charlie Harbin: p. 8;
    Charlie Harbin: p. 13
Photolibrary: Tony Anderson: cover
George Roos, Peter Arnold Inc./Science Photo Library:
    p. 5
Shutterstock: Medvedev Andrey: p. 4 (screw); Andrjuss:
    p. 4 (wedge), 31; Julián Rovagnati: p. 4 (inclined plane);
    Harley Molesworth: p. 4 (pulley); Wiktor Bubniak: p. 9;
    Suzanne Tucker: p. 20; Natalia Bratslavsky: p. 21

Library and Archives Canada Cataloguing in Publication

Christiansen, Jennifer
    Get to know wedges / Jennifer Christiansen.

(Get to know simple machines)
Includes index.
ISBN 978-0-7787-4470-2 (bound).--ISBN 978-0-7787-4487-0 (pbk.)

    1. Wedges--Juvenile literature.
I. Title. II. Series: Get to know simple machines

TJ1201.W44 C47 2009   j621.8   C2009-900850-5

Library of Congress Cataloging-in-Publication Data

Christiansen, Jennifer.
    Get to know wedges / Jennifer Christiansen.
        p. cm. -- (Get to know simple machines)
    Includes index.
    ISBN 978-0-7787-4487-0 (pbk. : alk. paper) -- ISBN 978-0-7787-4470-2
(reinforced library binding : alk. paper)
    1. Wedges--Juvenile literature. I. Title. II. Series.

TJ1201.W44C565 2009
621.8--dc22

                                                2009004902

Crabtree Publishing Company

www.crabtreebooks.com   1-800-387-7650

Published in Canada
Crabtree Publishing
616 Welland Ave.
St. Catharines, ON
L2M 5V6

Published in the United States
Crabtree Publishing
PMB16A
350 Fifth Ave., Suite 3308
New York, NY 10118

Published in the United Kingdom
Crabtree Publishing
White Cross Mills
High Town, Lancaster
LA1 4XS

Published in Australia
Crabtree Publishing
386 Mt. Alexander Rd.
Ascot Vale (Melbourne)
VIC 3032

Contents

What is a Simple Machine?

All people have jobs to do. Some jobs take a lot of **energy**. Energy is the ability to do **work**. Simple machines help people get jobs done without working too hard. This is called **mechanical advantage**.

Simple machines are **tools** that are made up of very few parts. There are six kinds of simple machines. They are **inclined planes**, levers, pulleys, **wedges**, screws, and wheels and axles.

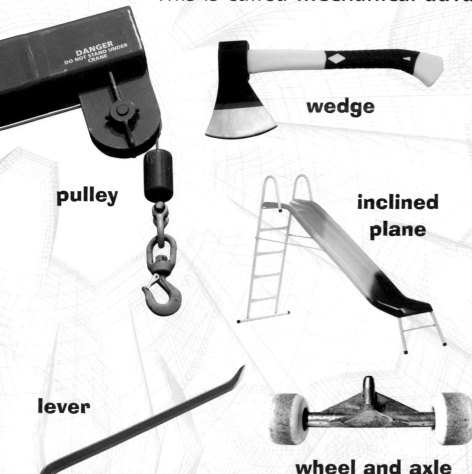

pulley

wedge

inclined plane

lever

wheel and axle

screw

These pictures show an example of each kind of simple machine.

A wedge is one kind of simple machine. A wedge is made up of two inclined planes. The two inclined planes meet to form a point. A wedge is used to pull things apart.

You may have seen wedges such as a chisel, an axe, and a door stop.

Arrowheads are examples of wedges used by people long ago.

Test Out the Wedge!

Use your energy to put each of these wedges to work. Watch how the clay moves when you use wedges.
You will need:

fork

screwdriver

scissors

lump of clay

Roll the clay into a ball. The ball should be about as large as a softball.

Use your fork and poke it into the clay. What happens to the clay when you lift up your fork?

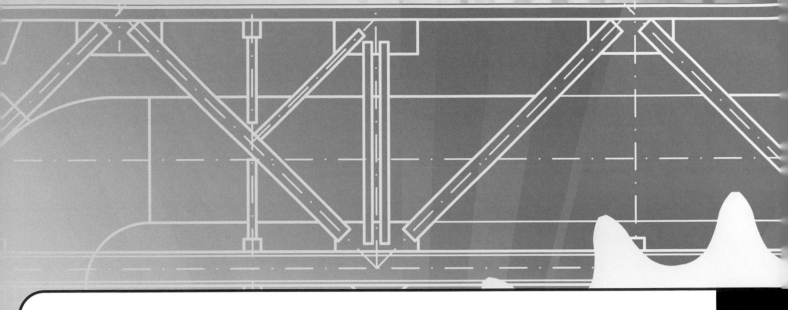

Roll the clay ball so that it is in motion. Have a friend hold the screwdriver in the clay's path. What did the screwdriver do to the clay ball?

Roll the clay into any shape you wish. Use the scissors to cut the clay. How did the clay change?

Wedges vs. Inclined Planes

Wedges are shaped like inclined planes. But the work they do and how they do it is different. Inclined planes, such as stairs and ramps, stay in one place. Unlike inclined planes, wedges need **force** to work. A shovel is one kind of wedge. In order to work, the shovel's thin edge must be forced into the dirt. Without force, the shovel wouldn't be able to get the job done.

To have a pancake breakfast, we need this wedge and force to flip over the pancakes.

An axe is a type of wedge that loggers use to cut wood.

Wedge It!

Try to move two books apart using a wedge and an inclined plane. You will need:

two books

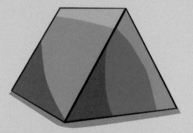

triangular block

Step 1

Place two books side by side with their bindings touching each other.

Step 2

Put the thin edge of the block in between the two books.

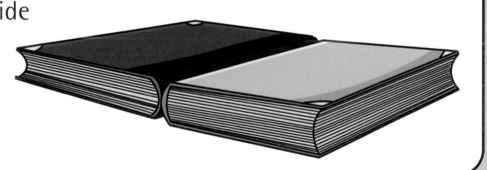

Using force at the top of the block, push the block down between the two books.

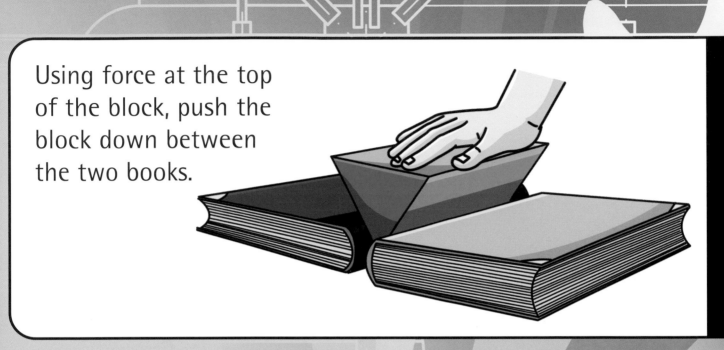

Think about what happened when you added force to the block. What would have happened to the books if you didn't add force?

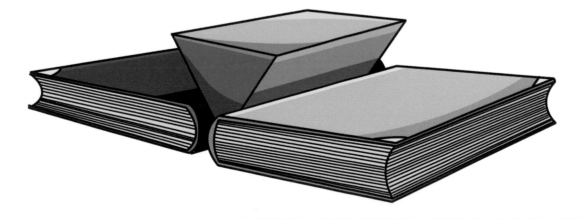

Single Wedges

There are two kinds of wedges: **single wedges** and **double wedges**. Single wedges have only one **slope** and are placed flat on the ground. Most single wedges are used to stop things from moving. A door stop is a single wedge.

Wheel blocks are another single wedge. They stop a car's wheels from moving. The thin edge of the wheel block is put under the wheel with the slope and thicker part of the wedge moving up and away.

This door stop is a single wedge. It stops the door from closing.

This wheel block keeps the car from rolling forward.

Many workers need wheel blocks to get their jobs done safely. Mechanics count on this single wedge to keep cars and trucks in place.

Stop It!

See if you can stop a moving door with a single wedge. You will need:

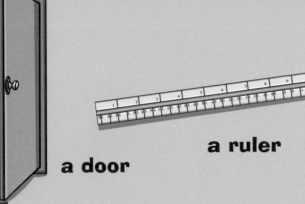

a door

a ruler

a friend

Take turns swinging a door back and forth to create motion.

What can you do to make the motion stop? Try using a ruler as a single wedge to stop the door from closing.

Step 1

Step 2

Place the ruler so that the bottom edge is on the floor and moves at an upward angle away from the doorway.

Have your friend gently swing the door closed while you hold the ruler in place. What happens to the moving door?

Step 4

15

Double Wedges

Noses of airplanes, knives, and sewing needles are all double wedges. Instead of having one slope like single wedges, they have two.

Double wedges are made up of two inclined planes on their sides. The front of the tool has a long, thin edge. The slopes of the inclined planes face outward and get wider toward the back of the tool. An axe is one kind of double wedge. Once someone swings its thin edge into a tree, the force used to push the axe into the trunk begins to move outward in two directions making a cut. Timber!

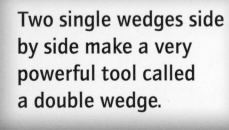

Two single wedges side by side make a very powerful tool called a double wedge.

Double Wedge   Single Wedge

Chuck Yeager's airplane, the *Bell X-1*, was the first plane to fly faster than the speed of sound. The nose of his plane was a double wedge that cut the air, making a loud boom!

Chuck Yeager nicknamed his plane "Glamorous Glennis," after his wife.

Tower Demolition!

Use your own body to make a powerful double wedge. You will need:

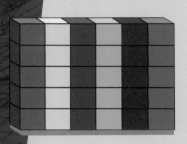

30 blocks

hands

Begin by stacking your blocks up and out to build a tall, wide tower.

Use one hand as a single wedge. Using force, push your hand into the center of the tower. How many blocks came down?

18

Step 1

Step 2

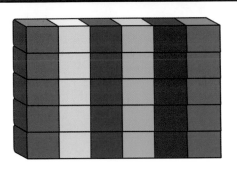

Now put your hands together with your palms touching. You have made your own double wedge.

Just like step two, use force to drive your double wedge into the middle of your tower. Count how many blocks you knocked down this time. Which wedge worked better to knock down the tower?

Wedges in Motion

Wedges need force to make a job easier. The more **power** used to force a wedge into an object, the easier and faster work will be. This is called mechanical advantage. The less power force has, the harder and slower work will be.

Very big wedges such as the **bow** (the front) of a boat need a lot of power to move through the water. Small wedges such as teeth can cut through food using just a little power. When these pushing forces are used, they help wedges move things to the side that are in the way.

Moving this snow would be hard without a shovel and some power behind it!

This boat needs a lot of power to move its bow through the water.

Early snowplows were rollers pulled by horses through the snow. Snow was flattened, not scraped up. Now wedges are used to move the snow.

21

Use Your Power!

To stop motion, split, and poke things you can use the wedges found on your body. You will need:

your body

an apple

a toy car

some clay

Step 1

Use force to roll a toy car across the floor. Find a way to use your hand as a single wedge to stop its motion.

Step 2

Hold an apple. Use your teeth as a double wedge to pierce it or cut it open.

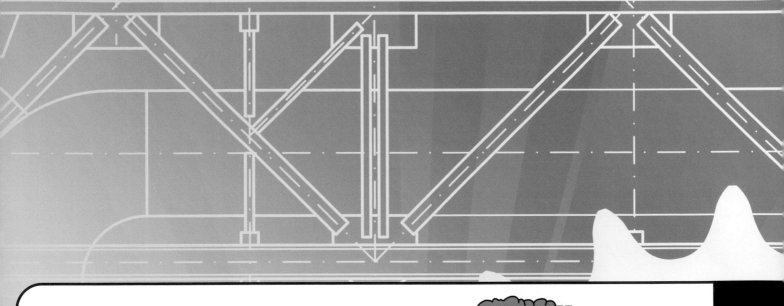

Bite down with just a little power. What happens? What happens when you add more power to your wedge?

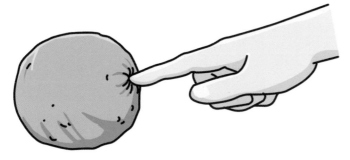

What happens when you use more and less power to poke your clay?

Roll your clay into a ball. Use the point of your finger as a double wedge to poke a hole into the clay.

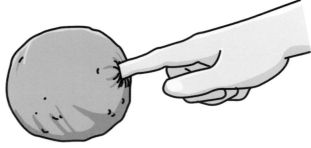

Wedges in Action!

At work and at home, people use wedges to get their work done with less **effort**. When you are eating, the force you give a fork helps to pick up food and carry it to your mouth.

Wood-carvers use chisels that they force into wood. When they do this, the wood they do not want is pushed away by the wedge. Even football players line up in a wedge. This helps them block the other team.

This chef is taking his pizza out of the oven with the help of a wedge.

The cowcatcher stops things from hitting the wheels of the train.

This train has a wedge called a cowcatcher. It was invented to move rocks and trash off the track as the train was moving.

Be an Artist!

You can be like a wood-carver too!

You will need:

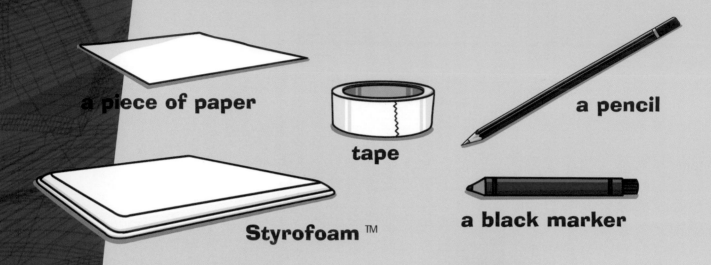

a piece of paper

tape

a pencil

Styrofoam ™

a black marker

Step 1

Draw a simple picture on your paper. Do not use too many details.

Step 2

Tape your paper to the top of the piece of Styrofoam.™

Use your pencil to trace over your drawing. Be sure to use enough force so that you are carving the picture into the Styrofoam.™

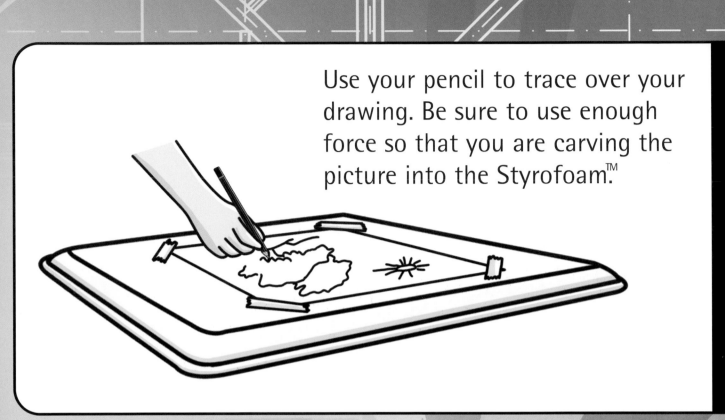

Take your paper off of your Styrofoam™ to see what you made. Your pencil was a wedge. It pushed the Styrofoam™ to the side and made space for your picture.

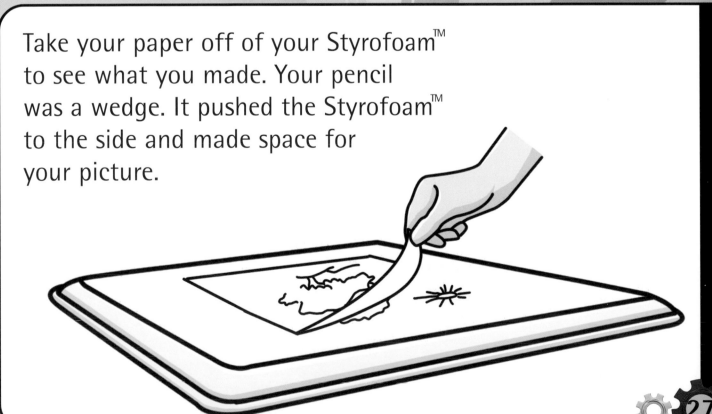

Working Together

Wedges help us get work done. Wedges can also make our jobs faster and easier. When we put wedges together with other simple machines, they make a **complex machine**.

A plow is a complex machine. Wedges on a plow move dirt and make holes to plant seeds. Long ago, farmers used big shovels pulled by animals to do this job. Putting wedges together with wheels and axles made their job much faster and easier.

When you add wheels and axles to these wedges, this plow becomes a complex machine.

Plows are complex machines that use wedges to move soil.

The earliest plows were invented by the Egyptians. They tied the ropes from their plows to the horns of oxen to make their work easier.

29

Glossary

bow The front of a boat

complex machine A machine where two or more simple machines work together

double wedge Two back-to-back inclined planes used to split objects apart

effort Force or physical energy given to a simple machine

energy The use of force to do work or move an object

force Something that changes the motion or rest of an object

inclined plane A flat or level surface set at an angle

mechanical advantage How much easier and faster a machine makes your work

power The speed of work

single wedge An inclined plane used to stop motion

slope How steep a distance is

tool A simple or complex machine we use to make work easier and faster

wedge A simple machine used to cut, poke, pull things apart, or stop motion

work The amount of force used over a distance

Index

Web Sites

www.edheads.org/activities/simple-machines/

teacher.scholastic.com/dirtrep/Simple/wedge.htm

www.sciencetech.technomuses.ca/english/schoolzone/Info_Simple_Machines2.cfm#wedge

www.brainpop.com/technology/simplemachines

www.mikids.com/Smachines.htm

www.coe.uh.edu/archive/science/science_lessons/scienceles1/finalhome.htm

Printed in U.S.A — CG